Radar

Radar Riders

Robin and Chris Lawrie

Illustrated by
Robin Lawrie

Acknowledgements

The authors and publishers would like to thank Julia Francis, Hereford Diocesan Deaf Church lay co-chaplain, for her help with the sign language in the *Chain Gang* books, and Dr Cathy Turtle, ecologist, for her help with the selection of species in books 13 to 18.

Published by Evans Brothers Limited
2A Portman Mansions
Chiltern Street
London W1U 6NR

© Robin and Christine Lawrie
First published 2004

Printed in Hong Kong

British Library Cataloguing in Publication data.
Lawrie, Robin
  Radar Riders. – (The Chain Gang)
  1. Slam Duncan (Fictitious character) – Juvenile fiction
  2. All terrain cycling – Juvenile fiction 3. Adventure stories
  4. Children's stories
  I. Title II. Lawrie, Chris
  823.9'14[J]

ISBN 0 237 525607

Hi, my name is 'Slam' Duncan.

I ride and race downhill mountain bikes with a group of friends. We call ourselves 'The Chain Gang'.

I'm Fionn.

I'm Aziz, known as DOZY.

I'm Larry.

We practise and race on a big hill called Westridge behind our village. But a property development firm has bought the hill and plans to build houses right across our best courses. They've said

we can still race there, but not where they want to build.

(*I'm Andy. (Andy is deaf and signs instead of talking.)

5

We had to persuade the race organizers to build a new course. But where? The only place was through an old quarry.

Trees had
fallen into it.
Old cars had been pushed
into it, together with lots of old
junk. Boulders had broken off the side.
What a mess.

7

Later, on the internet, we checked out a website called 'West Coast Biking' from the North Shore of Vancouver, in Canada.
It gave us lots of ideas about building courses in difficult places.

We printed a few out.

The next Saturday we started planning our new course. We could hardly walk it! How were we going to ride it?

Bit by bit we analysed the problems.

It wasn't going to be impossible after all.

But where were we going to get the wood to build all these ramps and flyovers? The answer lay at the bottom of the quarry.

We explained our ideas about the new course to the race organizers. They loved it. The following Saturday we got to work. Some older riders helped us.

First we built 'the ramp' . . .

. . . then 'the flyover' . . .

. . . then the 'corkscrew'. . .

It took a few weekends, but at last
it was done . . .

. . . and we were . . .

13

At least, some of us were.

Larry and Andy were having problems with the 'North Shore' sections.

Andy kept working at it, but Larry completely lost  his bottle. He talked to Dozy who knew some sports psychology. Dozy had heard it all before. He was really fed up with hearing it.

Look, Larry, sports psychology isn't going to help on this. It's a tough course, you just need to work hard and learn it.

I said I'd help him, so that evening . . .

OK, Larry, don't brake here or you'll slide off.

OH NO!

. . . but he didn't listen.

A few minutes later, while he was recovering . . .

Wow! Look at that! Lesser horseshoe bats!

Their eyes are not too good but they have fantastic hearing. They make high pitched squeaks that bounce off objects around them and go back to their ears.

So we did. Dozy's a whiz with computers.
I asked him if he could invent
something to help Larry 'see'
the course better.

Larry had to get home early.

Bye, Larry! I'll text you if I find an answer.

Then as we were walking back through Dozy's dad's shop . . .

Hey! I wonder if . . .

It was a digital security camera.

Dad's away tomorrow and the shop'll be shut, so he'll never miss it.

He got his helmet and some tape . . .

OK, meet me on Westridge tomorrow.

Next day, at the top of the course.

Dozy and I were ready to go.

He wouldn't tell me why, he just said he was trying to help Larry with his problem.

So off we went.

Dozy had told me not to get more than five metres in front of him.

I took it smooth and steady – especially the corkscrew. It was a good run.

We saw Andy come down behind us. He was practising on his own. That evening we replayed the run on Dozy's computer.

Perfect!

COOL!

First Dozy went to the video editing
program on his computer. Next he
downloaded the digital video of my run.
Then he added a backing track and
sound effects from his keyboard

Dozy played
the video through.
Whenever there was a big rock he stopped
the film and inserted a 'bleep' on track
two. If there was a root, he put in a
'bloop'. For a right hand bend
a 'niaow'. For a left, a 'vweep'.

A braking point was 'skreetch', a jump was 'wheee'. At last the video was finished and we texted Larry.

Strange, how can you 'see' an MP3?

Larry soon found out.

WOW!

KACHOONGA-KACHOONGA-BLEEP BLEEP-
NIAOWW KACHOONGA KACHOONGA VWEEP
WAAOOP KACHOONGA-KACHOONGA VWEEP
BLOOP-KACHOONGA-KACHOONGA-BLOOP
WHEE-VWEEP-WHEE-KACHOONGA-KACHOONGA
WAOOOP-BLOOP-BLEEP-KACHOONGA KACHOO...
CHOONG

We must have watched the video a dozen times or more until the new course was completely burned into our brains. Then . . .

Larry did as he was told.

He listened to the MP3

everywhere he went.

Yes, everywhere!

Finally he was ready to ride the course bat-style, using his ears not his eyes.

Down the ramp . . .

Dozy was so chuffed with the tape he started thinking about being a sound engineer instead of a sports psychologist. He added some vocals to the backing track. It sounded very professional. Just for laughs, we emailed it as an MP3 to a late-night DJ on Radio Shredshire.

Alright all you nightowls out there in radioland. got a new track called 'Radar Riders' by a new name 'Batman' Dozy - it's gonna be a smash!

HIT IT, BATMAN!

We could not believe our ears!

'Radar Riders' was a hit! For a week or two you heard it everywhere . . .

. . . especially on the new Westridge course. Word had got out and everybody knew what 'Radar Riders' was about . . .

. . . including the race marshals!

Then on the morning of the race . . .

KERRASH!

WALLOP!

OW!

Overnight, the marshals had changed
several corners.

Dozy's record made the course too easy.

So we moved things
around a bit.

We'd brainwashed ourselves
with the whole
Radar Rider and
'seeing with our ears' bat thing, and now
we only had two hours to practise the
new course. Larry had slept in –
as usual. No practice
for him. He got to
the start just in time
for his run. There was no time to tell him
about the changes to the course.

START

Hey, hang on!

You can guess what happened. At the
first corner Larry went 'vweep', when he
should have gone 'niaoww'!

OH NO!

Most of us got to the bottom. But with very slow times. Andy was the last to come down. And he was fast.